THE HIDDEN WINGS

Pushpa Nalavade

BookLeaf
Publishing

India | USA | UK

Presentation by *BookLeaf Publishing*

Web: www.bookleafpub.com

E-mail: info@bookleafpub.com

ISBN: 9789363317895

First edition 2024

Thanks to this life, the situations and the people in it!

ACKNOWLEDGEMENT

I would like to express my heartfelt gratitude to my parents, my family and friends for the person I am today. A special mention to my school English teacher- Roopali Mitra ma'am, who inspired me during my growing-up days and made me fall in love with the English language.

I believe in the power of continuous evolution, striving each day to become a better version of myself.

I am inspired by this quote from Emily Dickinson:

"That it will never come again is what makes life so sweet."

PREFACE

Since childhood, I've been chronicling my daily musings in a diary.

Occasionally, these musings morphed into poetic verses. This collection serves as a testament to my varied experiences and reflections, resonating with readers navigating their own emotional landscapes.

As you delve into these pages, a revelation dawns: hidden within you are wings yearning to take flight, transcending the confines of perception to embrace boundless possibilities.

INDEX

1. MOTHER

God made her special, you see,
And then, oh so kindly, she made me.
She helped me come into this bright world,
And smiled at me as my life unfurled.

I reached up my hands, small and slight,
And she hugged me close with all her might.
The love and warmth I feel with her,
Is so big and sparse, it makes my heart purr.

When I trip, my knees go "Bang!"
She's right there, with a hug and a hand.
She helps me up and wipes my tears,
Makes my scrapes and my fears disappear.

Her laughs are mine, and so are her tears,
Her love is magic that never disappears.
Her heart is a pot, full and brimming,
With love so deep, it keeps on giving.

She feeds me, cares without any end,
So, with all my heart, thanks I send.
Oh, Mom, you're my hero and I love you!
From my head to my toes,
more than you'll ever know!

2. LIFE

Life is a vibrant rainbow...
A spectrum of colors, bold and bright.
Each hue a story of beauty,
Revealing life's secrets, day and night.

Life brims with joy and laughter,
A dance of delight mixed through.
Yet, shadows of sadness
will chase away the sun,
Reminding us that sorrow touches everyone.

Life mirrors everything we feel,
Reflecting both the bitter and the sweet.
At times it stirs a storm of fear,
Leaving us to wrestle with defeat.

Life is often wet with tears,
Tears of joy, tears from pain.
Fear for challenges yet to be faced,
And the tears that mingle into the rain.

Yet still, life is beautiful and diverse,
It flows like a river, relentless and free.
Embrace all it offers, ride through its course,
And find peace, where your worries cease.

Bright and serene as you face the sun every morning,
Quite and peaceful as you rest on the bedside,
Enjoy the moments of love and joy
Forget the time of jealousy and envy
Embrace the moment in its true colors...
When your soul alone retreats....!

3. RIVERSFLOW

River's gentle flow, a mirror of our living.
Each ripple is a tale, each current forgiving.
As rivers merge, so do our souls unite,
In friendship's embrace, in love's soft light.

Yet time's steady march brings subtle change.
Like rivers joining oceans, rearranged.
In meetings, we seek solace and relief.
Yet sometimes, obstacles sow disbelief.

A new course for the river, a shift in tide.
Similarly, confusion tests our strides.
In rivers, streets of water weave,
In us, tears and blood, are the cost we grieve.

A splash in the river, a clash of souls.
Isolation follows as darkness unfolds.
Alone we wander, desperate for a hand,
In this vast world, where do we stand?

The river, resilient, flows on its own
Yet a person alone feels deeply alone.
So cherish the connections, that keep us strong,
For together we weather whatever comes along!

4. CRIES OF THE SEED

Help! Help! a tiny seed did plead,
"Don't bury me here, I cannot breathe,"
Trampled beneath indifferent feet,
Lost in the shadows of the street.

I feel disgraced, this isn't my creed,
For I am the bearer of life indeed,
The silent feeder of their need,
From which their countless hunger feeds.

Yet, buried deep, I did not die,
Nor did I cower, or fear the sky.
The storms that raged and drenched my coat,
The scorching suns that set afloat,
None shook my core, nor made me sigh,
For Nature's hands craft, sculpt, and ply.

I embraced the dance of rain and light,
The eternal spin from day to night.
In nature's cryptic grand design,
Where growth is but a silent sign.

My form was split, my heart was torn,
Yet from this pain, new life was born.

Unseen, I thrived, beneath the loam,
In that dark earth, I found a home.

And as I pushed through the soil to the sun,
A tapestry of life was spun.
Given names by those who reap,
Unaware of the promises I keep.
They use me as they will, and when,
Unknowing that I'll rise again.
For I am crafted by Nature's hand,
A vital thread in her vast plan.

I am the seed, born of the land,
Destined to grow, to feed, to stand.
So heed the whispers of the seed.
Respect the life that lies in need.
For I am more than soil and shell,
In every heart, I'm meant to dwell.
As cycles turn and seasons sway,
In Nature's arms, I'll always stay.
A testament to her endless play
"I am creation, I am the way.!"

5. MONEY

Some people worship it, while others just curse,
Some kill for it, others die even worse.
That's the strange and funny truth,
Such is the mighty power of money's ruth!

Headlines Yell "A house was burgled",
News tells us "Two lives were robbed".
Radio talks of taxes that climb,
TV shows elections,
All because of a dime,
For what it's worth as it shines.

Why all this fuss?
It's plain to see- Money's at the heart, the key.
Money, they say, can do so much,
Bad when it crushes the life as such,
The feelings, the emotions, everything we see.

With money, you're a hero, stand so tall,
Without it, you're nothing, none at all.
It's ridiculous, it's funny,
That's the crazy power of money!

Money, Money, Money, no longer a joke.
Money, Money, Money, everyone's hope.
Chased like treasure, sweet as honey,
That's the endless pull of money!

6. THE LIGHT

Grant me strength, bestow me courage,
So I may labor in your mighty garage.
Equip me with tools, and guide my hand,
So I may stand tall, where others oppose.

Illuminate my path with your radiant light,
Show me the way that is just and right.
Help me sweep away the remnants of my past,
Clearing the way for peace that will last.

Gift me the joy that follows triumph's climb,
Bestow me with talents rare and sublime.
Grant me tranquility for clarity's sake,
Provide me purpose, my mark to make.

Guide me to discover the truest me,
And in my quest, O God, please bless me.
For I want to be the light,
with whatever my might.
And I want to glide,
with smoothness in every sight.

Be by my side, to help me ponder,
For it's not going to be easy,
To manoeuvre from dark to light!

7. TEENAGE

Teenage feels like a fleeting flight
A battle you face that never repeats.
It slices through life, sharp as a knife,
Gone in a flash, filled with both
strife and delight.

It's like a morning jog, shrouded in fog,
Mysterious, dim, yet stirring within.
Some boast of entering this phase with ease,
Trying to scare off ghosts that never cease.

Romance awakens, sweet melodies play,
Songs touch the heart, fiery in their sway.
Singing erupts, a soulful echo,
Voices rise freely, emotions aglow.

They say, "Love isn't all there is to life,"
Yet without love, what is life's strife?
Life without love barely seems alive,
For love fuels the days as we strive and thrive.

Teenage must yield to the age of old,
As buds bloom and wilt, truths unfold.
Marriage doesn't guarantee love's shine,

It might grow stronger over a long, winding
time.

One heart leads to another in this game,
Some connections deepen,
while others stay the same.
When you find yourself in life's deep trough,
Search for true love, soft and aloft!

8. THE DESIRE

I swear by the Almighty above,
To cling to hope, to nurture my love.
I have a path, a vision so clear.
Driven by desire, ambition O' dear
A heart ablaze, a restless mind,
Shining uniquely, one of a kind.

My faith whispers through the dark,
"This gloom shall not always mark
Your days, your times, your age...
Blame not the stage, just turn the page.
From shadows shall emerge a light,
Your unique fame, pure and bright."

Though trials arise and challenges loom,
Such moments of struggle are not our doom.
Wait for the day when joy takes flight,
When happiness dawns, radiant and bright.
The perfect time will come, it's true,
On your path wide, in skies blue.

My belief is firm, nature's course is wise:
Endure now, for sweet rewards shall rise.
From raw beginnings to ripened ends,
From bitter tastes to amends.

Both small and great, slow and swift,
Memories hold past gifts.

Life follows a timeless rule,
From past to present, it's nature's tool.
A journey from then, to now, to more,
Touching my soul, to the very core.
This truth I'll hold, never to sever,
Forever changed, I shall forget, never!

9. SUNSET

A single thought on a lonely path,
While the streets lay empty, uncrossed,
A glance from the crowd, subtle and mild,
With no meaning to fear, no stakes involved.
When love consents, words need not be
exchanged.

A lone cloud drifts across the sunny skies,
While the heavens around
remain brilliantly clear.
A shadow casts over the bright expanse,
Out of place in the vibrant cheer,
When the skies are blue and the earth celebrates.

A single wish at the edge of the day,
While the ground feels solid,
emotions are so tender.
A sigh touches a face, serene and open,
Destined to fade like the light of the setting sun,
When dusk falls, the day is transformed,
not ended.
That memory of the sunset is always shielded!

10. NIGHTINGALE

She fluttered gracefully,
from branch to branch.
Settling where comfort found her,
regardless of safety or peril.
The same diligence applied,
whether the perch proved secure or fraught.

Each pause brought fleeting joy,
her own solace, paramount
regardless of the world's concern.
Perched in quiet repose,
she reflected on past journeys...
the arduous paths and trails endured,
each struggle bolstering her resolve,
fruitful or not.

There she sat,
gathering strength and steadfastness,
fueling her spirit for the journeys ahead.

Her rest, a treasure chest of energy,
her resilience, a cherished asset
poised for the breaking dawn,
readying her for flights anew
towards horizons brightly lit!

11. RIPPLES

Sometimes confusion spirals,
taking unexpected turns,
Sending ripples coursing inward
and outward alike.
At times, the very notion of unsureness tires us,
Breeding misunderstandings
that echo far and wide.

Often, these moments forge peculiar distances,
A sense of separation, felt from deep hearts end

It's rarely a physical divide,
But rather, an emotional unraveling,
Where feelings stretch thin and control slips,
Difficult to maintain the essence of equilibrium .

Indeed, emotions hold their sway,
They chart the course through a tangled fray...
Confusion, gaps, misunderstandings deep,
They guide us where the shadows creep.

12. MOOD

Here, I stand in unfamiliar lands,
Yet everything is the same, bland and tame.
It's odd here, it just ends in a yawn.

The dining scenes, the meals between,
Menus unfold, soups served cold.
All mirrors of the past, except my restless mood.

Streets and roads, routine loads,
Sweet gestures at meetings and greets,
All so familiar, finely tuned,
Yet it feels different, traces assumed.
Simple it seems, to mingle and jest,
A light, easy treat, in theory, at best.

Faces in flux, polite and composed,
I'd shout from the depths if only I dared.
It's high time now, for fresh air, for escape,
From this cycle, this echo, this familiar shape!

The same old atmosphere, the same fake people
Topics unfurls, jabs at some, why the disgrace?
All the musings and the sorts that I hate to
participate in, as I want to play in my own
mood!

13. PARADISE

You are going away...
when I wanted you.
To the farthest of lands,
to the places I visited once...
and left my memories behind.

You are making your way through,
and making them alive...
to rekindle my thoughts,
and my feelings.

Making me realize,
pausing my thoughts,
refreshing my mind,
that how badly I wanted you,
then,
now,
and forever be!

14. MYSTERY

It opened as a book unread,
the lines that said...
The truth and my breath,
the feelings at their full depth.

The mysterious chapters that had no end,
the words had their own pace,
timely set for the books that I read...
the lines at length, all unsaid.

Are you with me?
It opened with the hopes,
of a widespread path.
The lines went on...
to the saddening of thoughts...
at a continuous stretch...
the deepening chapters...
I wonder if it makes sense.

The words that marveled
the tie between them...
none knew the cause...
one read into another
it went on ahead...

Are you still with me?
I really wonder.
Did you reach even half?
I ponder!!

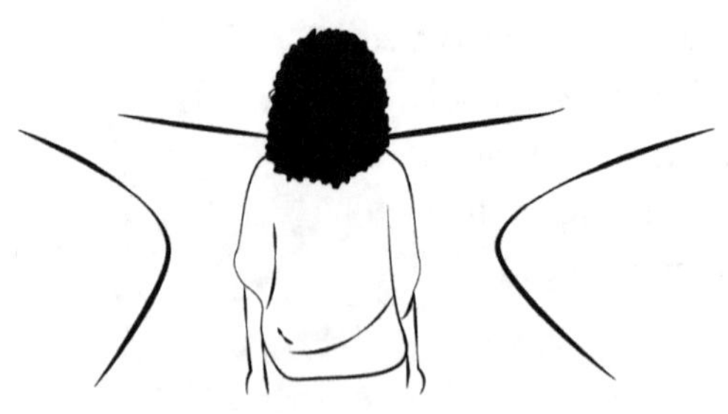

15. DREAMLAND

Thought and Thought
I thought a lot
Out of many a slot
I made a plot.
I wanted a balance,
while everything was silent.

My gospel. No one would hear.
Plans- cancel, could hardly bear.
My people - Is there anybody to part with?

It pierced directly into my heart.
My dreams?
What a tragedy!
They never were true.
Create dreams again.
Someone to lighten the dark.
It slowly started vanishing
was for no bothering at all.

The day never arrived
for I was longing.
whatever I thought was mine
but others belongings.

I cared for them,
lest they'll spoil the way.
Whatever I thought was best,
was taken away.

There was trouble all around
efforts proved futile.
For the irksome darkness was
bound to stay.
But then, 'I am going to face it."
I would say.

Emotions grew and spread
tears along the mounting threads
the feelings of the woefulness
leading me to ruthlessness.

I would imagine...
climbing the ladder of success
Gushing and surrendering down
I'd see again, holding the branches
with all its might.

All of a sudden something breaks
for I see, I am holding
The pen so tight
And my imagination vanishes
Just like the blink of an eye!

16. MOMENTS

When the path is clean, I don't cheer,
I just stare...
For the gusty winds are on their way,
to make it raw and bare.

When I am hurt, I don't cry,
I just close my eyes...
For pain, like the tide, ebbs and flows.

And when I am happy, I try not to laugh,
and observe my smile...
For true happiness is fleeting, a delicate wisp.

When I am sad, I don't look for the clown,
nor seek the colorful balloons...
For their smiles are painted,
Their laughter is an illusion.
And the air in them is just a whisk away...

And, when I am annoyed by life's many
vexations,
I do not flee, but wrap my eyes in darkness,
Embracing a moment's blindness.

When I cry, I do not let a tear touch my lips,
For I have tasted their bitter salt.

And when I am finally weary,
I do not seek solace
in the coziness of the loved ones,
for not only have they flown away afar
And choosing to be left alone...
For only in death does true rest reside.

17. VOICE

I wish...
I could do something...
But what?
Who knows?
Can you tell me?
No.
Why?
"Decide for yourself," said the voice.

Relax.
Collapse.
"No. You aren't a coward."
"Maybe I am?" I said.
"Why so?" asked the voice.
Brain.
Strain.
"Then train."

But how?
"Do it somehow."
Is there a way?
"Be gay and find the way."
Can I do that?
"Why doubt it?"

Go ahead.
"Be merry. Dont worry.
And don't be sorry."
But...
"No buts," said the voice.
"Do it as per your choice."

Wait, I said.
Who are you?
Who, me?
Yes, you.
I? Haha.
"It's you," said the voice.
Yes, it's me.
My deep voice.
No one else!

18. ALONE

Alone is the world, and so are we.
Amidst the momentary fun,
Where people wield great guns,
Everything has a price,
Even man's vice.

You see a lot,
Hear a shot.
You try, but whisper, "I cannot."
You witness a kill,
Watch bills climb high,
When a burglar strikes,
You do nothing but comply.

You feel wonder,
At the sight of a murder.
Boys seethe with anger,
While you grapple with hunger.
You don't use your skill,
Instead, you run on heels,
And let the mills stand still.

Do you know the feeling? You know it.
You do feel! You just won't admit it.

You see a dreadful sight,
But you prefer to escape.
People stand for votes,
Indifferent, until bribed with notes.

You witness a robbery,
And retreat quietly.
You avoid straining your brain,
Which might help some, but not all.
Instead, you flee and phone,
Help arrives,
When everything is gone,
Leaving only forlorn.

Authorities rushed in,
saying, "Don't worry."
For they cannot utter,
"We are sorry."
Nothing changes, except the hope,
You find nothing, seeking any scope.
You search around, and find no one,
Run helter shelter, seeking help.
None arrives, and you are broke
You are close to moments of discovery , and
bound to say,
"Alas, I am alone."

19. INCIDENCES

Incidences weave through our lives,
Realized and savored over time.
Each one reveals its depth,
Bringing myriad experiences,
Yet we survive around them.

To grasp their depth
Is neither easy nor unexacting.
Patience and prudence are essential,
Without which true mastery remains elusive.

Incidences must be felt
From the core of your own experience,
For they are unique and rare,
Shaping your outlook,
Guiding your attitude.

One day, you will foresee
Overcoming challenges
Stretching across the vast expanse
Of life's intricate drapery
Which is surely not easy and full of uncertainty
But you will be ready
To march ahead with fears unfolded!

20. THE RIDE

I kept striving hard,
To ascend to a height,
Where confidence and satisfaction collide.

But it all felt the same,
Wanting to go even higher,
To learn more about me and my surroundings.

But alas, the familiar monotony,
A yearning to soar further,
To stretch and explore,
To unearth more of my core.

At this juncture, I'm tangled and bemused,
Yearning desperately for a respite.
Yet, I pause and ponder,
They say 'Opportunities knock but once'.
And i'd say, what if I skip them for new?.

Why then, remain silent?
Forge ahead, seize the moment.
Yes! I leaped,
Reaching for even greater heights,
To a new, unexplored place.

The world offers so much,
For everyone to use and grow.
But in human-made controlled things,
Options are limited...
And not everyone gets a chance.

Being alert and taking action,
Not giving up, getting into the motion...
Starting things and staying involved,
Are what help us reach our objectives,
get it solved...

To build a strong foundation,
you need to surrender to devotion...
Where any challenge can be faced,
Proving if you have the will,
you have the notion...

For it to be your own,
It has to be your own creation!

21. THE RISE

Life was sheer hell, a relentless grind,
Devoid of zest, lacking rest.
Finding everyone hostile,
I began crafting my own profile.
Chagrined, yet no longer upset,
I believed in the sunrise after every sunset.

Certain of a brighter day,
I knew sorrows would be swept away.
The familiar surge of anger
Would be erased, leaving me stronger.
I slowly squirmed in my chair,
With utmost care in my movements there.

Filthy, sleazy, sick, and broken,
I clung to the basic needs, unspoken.
I knew I had to sow and reap,
To awaken from this painful sleep.
A direction emerged, clear and bright,
Freshness leads to newfound perfection.

One thing was sure: I grew higher,
Rising above my demarcations,
Fuelled by an inner fire!

22. OUR MEETING

You said something,
for people it meant nothing
But for me, it was everything
Something that created
An imbalance…
in the very silence of my life.

For a moment, it felt
as if life had been nurtured
Felt myself, captured
Was it that early?
My heart was still not mature.

You said all you could but relayed nothing
I was a silent statue, my lips of no value
Aghast I was, wondering like a zombie
Didn't you notice my state of mind?
No words. No sentences
We acted mute
but it meant everything.

Nobody knew we would meet
A chilling cold amidst the heat
I was pleasantly surprised
I got my seat and my heart swelled

The windy night and slippery road
Why on earth do we have to retreat?
We both knew it was indeed
the moment to breathe
embrace the moments to cheer and laugh
For we had just discovered,
Love at first sight!

Care and affection,
shared in each other's beneath
The place you gave me
You will see
I will keep
Only for you.
For you did say,
"Again, shall we meet!"

23. TOO LATE

To tell you that, I've fallen for you
Is a bit too late you see
And I don't know
How much this means to you.
But I've decided
I am going to let you know
Oh yes, Oh yes, I shall do.

To tell you that
My heart sings for you
Is a bit too late you see
And I don't know
Where my heart is?
But I am sure
You too have lost yours too
Oh yes. Oh yes, it indeed has,
I know it for you.

To tell you that
I've started thinking a lot these days
Is a bit too late, you see
I wish if you could
Realize this earlier…

To tell you that
I can't stay without you
Is a bit too late, you see
Because the time is ripe
It feels so bright
The sunrays kissing
And whispering in your ears
Traveling through the night.

Oh yes, Oh yes, That's the love
I have for you.
I am certain
That you know it too!.

24. YOUR PRESENCE

Every evening, I think about you
I long for you…
I want you to know how much I care.
I love you, I adore you.
Because when you are around
You make the dull so bright
Every moment I find myself with you,
The birds sing and the trees take pride.

Since the day I found you
I've started loving my own life.
I enjoy being alone
Lost in my mood, smiling.
I savor every second,
Every minute, and every hour.
But your absence steals it away.
It's all hidden in you
The real charm, the real hope.
You make me discern
What it is to live a life
with you, without you.
And you know what?
My life
I owe it to you!

25. WINDS OF TRUST

You gushed through like a wind
Blowing up all my worries
Your lovely questionnaire
Has left behind a patch of memories
You did give options
The answer is rare
Your confidence led me to say
I knew you would for sure, care.

Your statement has proved
So real and true
The idea behind me saying 'yes',
Stood nothing
But a symbol of trust
And a clue.

Your statement was a lovely surprise
I could never have made a guess
I am confident
You've understood my feelings
And a deep thought we share
It will prove to be a blessing
Because I trust you
And I trust your love.

26. THE ABSENCE

Your absence has made me grasp
All the differences you bring to life.
I've begun to understand
Your very own 'disappointments' and strife.

I feel myself losing control,
My eyes just blinking, waiting,
Hoping for someone
They know they won't come.
They've got to wait,
Not for long...
They've realized
Those moments are rare.

The brightness of the day
Darkens like a sullen dawn.
The cold, pleasant night
Remembers your smiling face,
Your lively talks, now fading,
Slowly becoming brown,
Replaced by blank stares.

For when you are gone,
Things aren't the same.!

27. THE DEPTH OF LOVE

Not the one I was earlier,
so unsteady and restless.
Unaware of the infant love
growing older, day by day.
I am not shy anymore,
and I have a confession.
No words can fully express
my feelings, worth so much.

Carefree and unafraid,
I have recently discovered,
my love has become an obsession.
No match until
I've realized,
your lips and the sun,
your love, the cool breeze.
I hope it never ceases.

Not that I was aware of the meaning
of life and death,
but your love
goes to such depths.
I cherish every breath.
And why wouldn't I?
That's my manifestation!

28. ETERNAL THOUGHTS

Your thoughts are so strong,
They can't be measured.
We just dined,
Had a lovely time,
But your remembrance
At this moment, is only prime.

The hills and beaches,
Beautiful and prolonged,
Nature's creativity at every furlong.
You don't have to create it,
You just feel it,
And it's a lovely time.
But your thoughts
In this hour, is only sunshine.

The villas and mansions,
Old and antique,
So beautiful,
People around
In a small boutique.
You don't have to say it,
For they hold a class of their own.

But your warm memories
Fuel my passion,
Unique and new,
I hope they linger forever.
You are around me,
Today and always,
In every moment after.

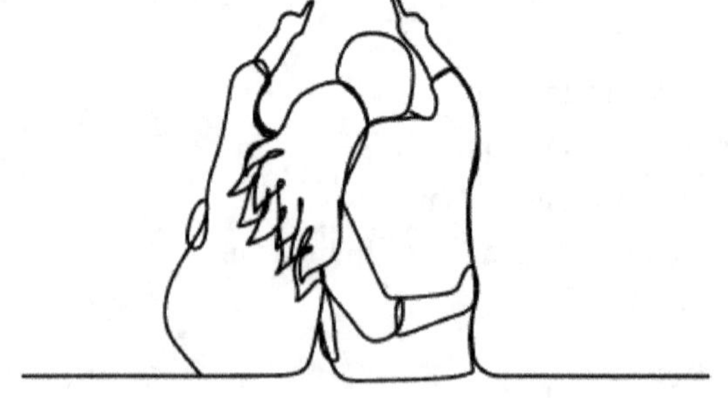

29. THE HEARTBEAT

Does the heart 'beat'?
If yes, so what?
A very natural process,
I had thought.
Birth, at its origin.
Childhood, at its ripening.
Maturity, at its margin.
The process went on and on.

Experience declared – go tread on.
The coolness of the blowing breeze,
The warmth of the hottest summer,
The unsteady laughter of the waves,
And the rumbling sound of the thunder.

I've experienced the rhythm of the heart,
The dripping music of the rain,
Summer, autumn, winter, spring,
Imagining the worth each season would bring.
The desperation, I don't care,
But I swear I wasn't aware,
The music from the heart-beating
Is my latest care.

30. DESTINY

Someone had inquired,
If I had asked?
Something on this auspicious day,
Something for my own.
Yes, I did say.
A new life, a new horizon
I have to step in…
Rather, I already have.

The choice is purely mine,
For all that I possess
Shall be somebody else's one day
Rather, it already has.
Someone had asked,
If I'd already decided?
Yes, I did say.

A new outlook, a new faith
I had never trusted
To an extent, unexplainable.
No looking back,
Rather, I've already reached too far
To embrace my very own
Destiny!

31. THE LONGING

I missed you once again,
So desperately, more than ever before.
Because of that extra warmth
You have in you,
I needed it once again, so eagerly,
More than ever before.

Because of that extra faith
I have in you.
I missed your hands and the lovely touch
So very badly,
More than ever before.

Because of that extra care you have in you,
I wanted you once again,
So wretchedly, more than ever before.

Because of the passionate memories
You have left in me,
I wanted you and all of yours
So seriously, that
I missed you all over again.

32. THE SILENCE

Quiet was the atmosphere, and so was I,
Unable to speak enough
To express my feelings.
Quiet were your reactions
On my arrival
And the same on my departure.

I couldn't stop my feelings
And I am not sure
they'll linger longer
To convey my anxiety,
Nor did you stop me.

Quiet was the panorama,
And so were you.
We couldn't take a chance
To express our feelings.
You did try to
Urge me to stay,
But the silence was serene,
Nothing is too sure.

Both were silent,
You and me,
The reason is just and pure.

Somehow, I did enjoy it,
For I understood its meaning.
In the cool, scenic atmosphere,
The need to remain
Quiet…
Was just so much more.

33. ALWAYS WITH ME

Don't you ever think
That I don't think about you.
You are always there,
A part of my soul,
Wherever I am,
You are with me.

I feel complete knowing
You live in me,
No matter how I am.

I know you understand
The depth of my feelings,
For there is nothing beyond
This love I cherish.

Don't you ever feel
That I don't care about you.
You are my only one,
The reason I sustain myself.

I am certain you know it by now
That even in your absence,
Your presence is felt
Throughout my mind,

My heart, my body,
And my soul.

34. BEING LOVED

It's a wonderful feeling,
To be needed,
To be expected.
It makes one realize
Their importance.

It's a heartwarming feeling,
To be wanted,
To be invited.
It makes one understand
Their significance.

It's a profound healing,
To be loved and cared for,
To love and care.
It reveals the beauty
Of surrender,
The value of love,
The sharing of trust,
The soothing power of affection.

It's truly, beautiful
To have you,
And to be yours.
I cherish this bond
With all my heart.

35. YOUR ARRIVAL

If I could choose for you
The kind of arrival you deserve,
The kind I dream for you,
From all the brightest days
Of all the years,
I would choose a day
As sunny as your smile,
As warm as your heart,
And as wonderful as you are.

Because you deserve it,
For all you've done for me.
I want you to believe,
To place your trust in me,
For everything I do,
I do it all for you.

Don't ever let
the sun to go down on me,
For I know, deep in my heart,
You are mine and only mine.

36. REFLECTION

Today, I don't know why,
But your memories are
Growing stronger and deeper,
Bringing a sudden fear of losing you.
Yet, your confidence
Is my only relief.

I find myself recalling
Your moves and your words,
Encroaching, blending with my own.
A sudden fear of forgetting them
Overwhelms me,
But your assurance
Is my steadfast belief.

I've started to understand
The people and society around us,
their ways and norms.
A sudden fear of repulsion
Lingers on their part.

But your care and our true moments
These are the only briefs we need.
Together, we must strive,
For today, tomorrow, and forever.

37. HOME

Tall are the buildings,
and so many people.
Cars and motorbikes—
Everyone is rushing.
Dig up the entire colony,
gather the lanes and the roads,
and bundle up all the streets.

Christmas trees and lights around,
Beautify the shops with all its might.
And jam up the entire city!
But no one can make homes
out of stones and sand,
piece by piece to greater heights,
with bricks and cement
and laborers abound.

Malls are plenty,
and things are in abundance.
Forests and mountains
call for a caress.
Nothing is astounding,
for the soul to breathe,
but the touch of your hand
and the way you make me feel—

that is the place in my heart
I want to make my home.
For home is where
I see you with me.
My peace and my solace
are in being together.
Nothing matters
if you are not in it—
the life,
the home.

38. STATE OF MIND

I kept trying hard
To reach a greater height
Where I can feel
Confident and satisfied.
But then,
The same old consistent crusade
craving to reach even further,
To stretch a little more,
To know myself better.

Yet, I realize
Opportunity comes
But once.
Why then, keep quiet?
Go ahead and try it out.

Yes! I committed myself
To reach a much greater height,
To a newer horizon.

But then,
Manmade resources
Are few to choose from,
A few gain while others lose
Opportunities are limited.

Alertness and an active mind
Initiation and participation
Are the keys to greater might
To create a self-built stand.

So, I surmise:
Make your base so strong
No one can break, no one can bend.
Make your mind
Worthy of earth, sand, and mountains.

Come what may,
You will stand tall,
Forever as you always wanted.

39. MY LIFE, MY WAY

I want to live the way I choose
My freedom, my voice.
I don't care of the judgement
The misunderstanding or a perception
For I know the impact of deception.
I give 'me' a fair chance
I know what is in me.
It's my life.

I do everything that brings me joy,
My time, my space
I welcome everyone's suggestions,
But act on my own terms.
I don't care about the gossip, the rumours.
I know the muck it brings with changing human
nature
I give them the liberty of losing me.
It's my Life.

I strive to fulfil my wishes
my ambitions.
While I give what I can
I know my limitations

For I have only so much
And that is precious for those dear to me
I decide when to relinquish
It's my Life.

I want to stay authentic with the ingenuity
And my belief and my actions
For it gives me space to be who I am
And not let slip to the oblivion.
I've had my share of experiences
The ups and downs of life and am glad.
I've seen life!

I was being used and I said stop.
I loved them all and then I said No
My heart saw the abuse
I said enough.
I choose the people to remain, and not to.
For it's a good feeling as you clean your space
for a fresh start, for a new perspective.
It's my life.

I want to be my realest
Weirdest to the core.
I don't care who get drawn away.
It's ok.

I won't allow my trust to be stolen any more.
It's my life…
My essence…
It's the way I am!!

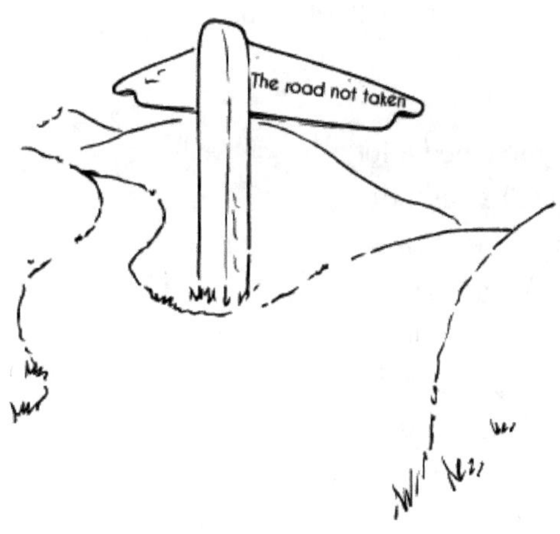

59

40. DAYDREAMING

I went on talking to myself,
Umm… and well… Ok Cut it out
someone there?
It's got to be!
Well, of course,
None but you.

I rambled on
non-stop chatter,
Excited?
No doubt, very well.
Done guessing. I'll tell you,
None but you.

I daydreamed a lot,
Thoughts cascading,
In a constant flow.
I'm all bananas,
I'm all tomatoes,
I'm all pineapples,
I'm all potatoes.
Ugh… it's too sweet!
Break!
The food we ate and the places we went
And thought a lot

Of our time spent well
And the things we did
Am I hungry?
Time for my luncheon!

Welcome, Welcome
Voices greeting
We are at an event
I am all excited
All eyes on us,
But my eyes are on you
Your smile sinks
you turn pink
I whisper
Why so shy?
You roll your eyes
A kiss on my cheek
I am on cloud nine
My eyes winking
Where are you?

41. TONIGHT

I don't wanna sleep tonight
And I need you to know
I must be the luckiest
Because my dream
Has come true.
I love someone wonderful
Someone, as good as you.

I love you,
Forever and again,
Sworn by my heart,
Unchanging and true.

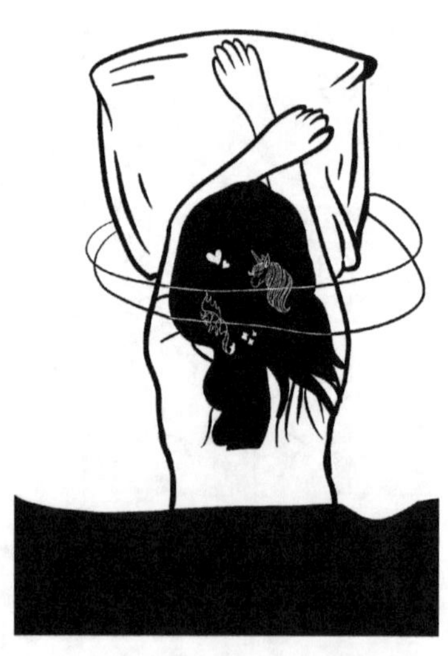

42. WHEN WE ARE TOGETHER

I wonder if the days could stretch a little longer,
Nights extend a little broader,
If time itself could pause its race,
I wish it could encircle
Whenever I am with you.

I wonder if the trees could stay evergreen,
Flowers with their colors serene,
The road we tread should never end,
I wish it could encompass
Whenever you are near me.

I wonder if the birds kept flying,
Fruits forever ripe and sweet,
The ever-floating gossamers,
I wish they could entwine
Whenever we gather together.

I wonder if the rain could shower forever,
Nature itself behaving
Against its nature,
Our closely-knit journey
Continuing endlessly,
I wish we could become one
Whenever we greet each other.

43. IN YOUR ABSENCE

There's nothing
I can immerse myself in to enjoy
Where are the things that once amused me?
Time passes by
Without a meaningful note.
There's no anticipation
for the evening to come
It's just as useless as the rest.
Where's the routine that made me feel wanted?

The people around are like
Unwanted weeds.
There's nobody I can talk to
Tell my thoughts or listen to theirs
Where have they all gone?
Those who once mattered?

I don't care, nor am I enchanted.
Everything around that once remained
Beautiful and alive
Where has it all disappeared?
They've promised a change
In their pattern,
At the very instance
Of your return.

44. THE WEIGHT OF WORDS

You said it once again,
And you've hurt me, O' dear,
Although you didn't mean a thing.

You treat me the best, I know,
You've given me the finest,
All that I could ever desire.
You know you are my only one,
With whom I share
My joys and sorrows,
And my so-called words,
Which I really don't mean.
You thought they were harsh,
But I know from the bottom of my heart,
They are in their truest sense,
Words I could ever share, to let you know
That I will be the last one
To ever hurt you
Or your feelings, and you better know.

You've made me apprehend
The little differences
That prevails here and there,
Which nowadays are usually rare.

I want you to understand
That these are the things
I expect the least from you.
I am very well aware
Your words have a way to sail,
Leaving me to ponder,
Like 'how?'

I am cornered,
I am given names,
I am hurt to the depths
I cannot express.

I want you to know
That small words
matter a lot.
Don't do this to me,
For I get weak and broken.
The impact is tremendous,
Leaving me motionless,
And my heart gets brittle.
The slightest touch
and it will fade away forever.

45. YOUR MAGIC

You don't anticipate
A thing…
When you know
What it's going to be.
You just think
It is there!

I need no assurance
When I know
What it's going to be.
I think, and you are there…
Everywhere!

You can't comprehend
Where my thoughts take me—
To the moon and back,
And deep in the oceans,
Where I want to lay bare
And no one can see.
A sudden click at my ear,
And I am here,
Exactly where I want to be!

46. WAITING FOR YOU

I want you to call me today,
For you didn't last night.
You don't know my state,
Unaware of the impact
Of your silence,
Your non-action.

I waited all night,
For you said you would come.
You don't know
what you took from me
Leaving me pale and hollow.
I want you to have it,
So, you understand
That my life is in your hands,
And you have to come.

I've been wondering
What will you bring?
If not my heart
I wonder
Doesn't it belong to me?
But it's also yours now
Let it be.
I want you to give yours to me

I ponder
Doesn't it belong to me?
I dare say, it's also mine
The shells of love
When together
They sing a song
In perfect harmony.

47. AWAITING REUNION

We parted ways
Lately,
For good or bad,
I am not sure.

Sadly,
You continue,
And so do I,
For we have no choice.

Slowly,
Things will change.
We both wait,
Anxiously,
For good and only good,
When we are together
once again.

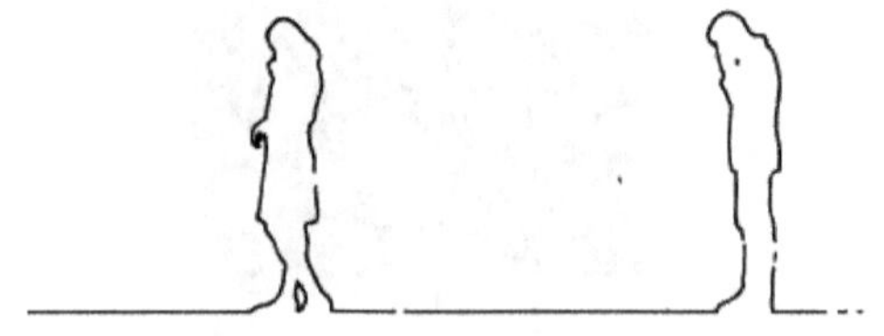

48. ELUSIVE MIND

I try to catch up with it,
It slips.
I try once again,
It topples once more.

It will never stay.
I try hard for it to remain,
It melts,
Flows away
To the unknown valleys.

The never-ending slope,
Difficult to ascend.
It's slippery,
It drives away.

I try my best to be with it,
It moves even faster.
I give up this time,
I'd rather say,
Flow with it
To the mysterious lands.

Hope did shine,
Now is the time

It moves ahead
I am compelled
Will you not stay?
My dear mind!

49. A CALL TO UNITE

It's time that we all unite
For a better cause
for a brighter light.

Let's keep our egos and their allies—
Emotions, attitudes, likes, and dislikes,
Favors and statuses—far aside
In our personal cupboards.
For they are temporary
They fade
As soon as you step outside.

It's time we rethink and give,
For all are equal in the eyes of God.
Let's put ourselves in others' shoes,
And see what they feel, think, and do.

Experience their good and bad phases,
Situations and circumstances,
The aura around...
And the times they dwelled.
The atmosphere that engulfs
Everyone around

Helps our lives for the better.
So don't just walk away
They are the ones that matter.
If they disappear,
So does the impact on our lives.

It's time that we all give up
The differences, the biases, and the alike.
Can we share our opinions
And rekindle thoughts?
And imaginations that are so far,
And yet so near, for our own
Easy to understand
and communicate with all.

For the world is changing
At a rapid pace
And we need to maintain the flow.
Then, there will be a smooth
and rapid response.
Free from bills and pills
Becoming a part of you.
For they bring both joys
and sorrows, too.
Life is like that
Up and down.
You don't need all that's out there
And you don't need a straight line.

50. THE ESSENCE OF BOND

Some bonds are different,
Unique in their own way,
True and serene.
They see no caste, no bar,
No age, no language,
Believing in the marriage
Of true minds
That is open and free.
They read each other, in all their worth,
A part of you,
Your very own.

Some bonds are confusing,
Difficult to understand,
To familiarize.
They carry along
Those who cherish their ways,
Their faith, their beliefs,
The dependence, the trust.
An understanding
That is difficult to part from,
Means so much to them
In all its worth.
For they become an insight into you,

As you are no different either,
And your very own.

Sometimes it's difficult to explain
And relinquish,
The things that never belonged
To either of the worlds.
But to a bond
That is rare, true,
And one of a kind.

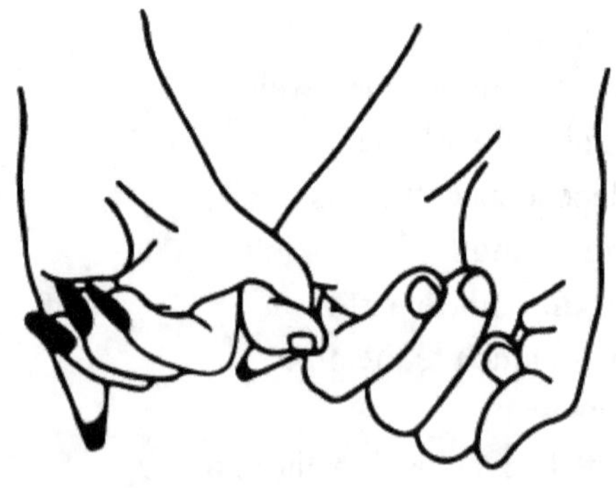

51. THE FRAGRANCE OF US

It's been so long since we asked ourselves,
Are we still the same?
Has it gotten lost,
The fragrance of truth,
Faith, and tranquility?

Let's unearth them,
The feelings that flow
To the extremity,
To the heights that once seemed
Impossible to imagine.

The path, it was the same,
Easy to follow and believe.
Yes, the colors are still the same,
The fragrance remains,
And so do we.

52. THE EVOLUTION

The pace has slowed,
To the point where,
Impatience turns slowly
Into patience.
Thoughts of innocence
Rise to heights of maturity,
Understanding the parameters
Of a relationship.

The race has held a steady pace,
Reaching conclusions as before.
The desire for a chance
This leads us down a path,
An arrow indicating
"Steady."

It plants itself,
For an in-depth study
To communicate,
To inhale
Every moment of this time.

53. THE DIALOGUE

I talk to you throughout,
With my heart wide open.
I want to share all things with you,
Including my talks
That doesn't concern you.
You don't enjoy them,
But you pretend so.
I know you have other things
To attend to,
So do I,
But I never let them come first.

I want to be part of everything,
With all my thoughts woven into you.
I want you to be aware
Of everything I have for you.
Even though
I'm not part of the show,
You have no time,
But you still encourage them.
I know your things are
More important,
But so are mine.
I want you to let them know.

I want time that is mine,
And only mine,
With you as a part,
And none other to start.
I want to draw the line in
The horizon, with
You, in the center,
And 'me' around it.
With a wish to reach you deeply,
If you don't mind.
You don't remain there,
No matter how much I strive.
You want me to stay,
Encircled and entwined.
Why don't you,
When I want you to be so?

54. THE JOURNEY

It was so easy,
Smooth and fine,
Our meetings and arguments,
Both crude and sunshine.
I wonder if they ever realized,
We were young but ripe,
Enough to shoulder
The burden of life
And the truth is divine.

It was so difficult,
Harsh and flat,
Our jokes and strokes,
Both high and bold.
I wonder if we ever realized
The hidden truth,
Both pain and agony,
That we faced bravely,
Enough to keep believing
There is laughter ahead,
Happiness and joy
Welcoming us
To a glorious future.

It was plain and simple,
At times non-relevant,
Yet we could discern
The meaning within.
We'd share the related
And discard the unwanted.
I wonder if they ever knew
The usefulness
Of our talks
That led us into
A path that enshrined.

It will be cherished
For now, and thereafter,
Forever I'd say,
For we know the warmth
And its true worth,
That gave us strength
And dictated its ways,
Rooting us in success,
Peace, and reality.

I wonder if anyone realized
The bond
That we have,
The relationship
We've maintained
For the years gone by
That has led us to thoughts

And imaginations
Difficult to perceive
And walkthrough
In the minds of ours,
Yet we do.

55. YOUR MOOD

Today, I am not in my usual mood,
Since the time I spoke to you last.

I'm all upset, the way things have moved,
Unexpected and wasteful,
The efforts I've put in,
From the last so many days,
To arrive at an understanding
That is best for us,
For they are needed now,
And only now.

This is the time,
I want you to change,
To let you know
What I have in store for you.
Not the way you took it,
And then your mood,
Since the time I spoke to you last.

You've made me think,
And reassure myself.
I am in two minds,
For the things I've done thus far,
Unfruitful and relentless.

Is there any outcome,
From start to end,
To make crisp conclusions,
Right for the moment
I am sure,
For they are meant for a change,
A change for good,
For you and me too.
But your mood,
Since the time I spoke to you last.

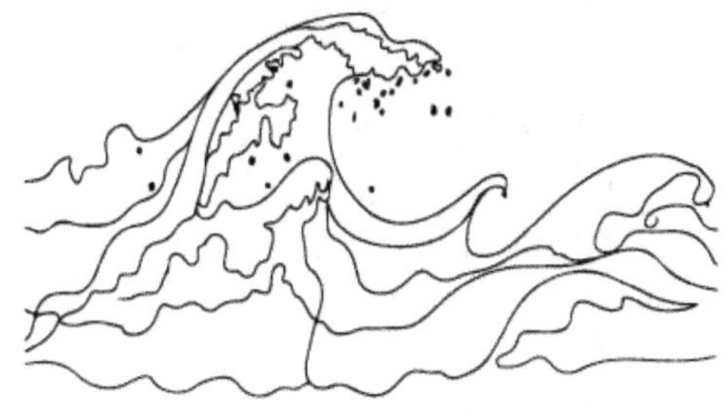

56. LAST NIGHT

Last night,
I was drenched in the rain,
Feeling its touch
Cold and wet on my cheeks.

The dew fell softly,
On the leaves,
Into the closed lips
Of petals still waking up.

In the soft murmurs of the heart,
I heard the music,
Two swans mingling,
Gliding to the long shores
Of a point of no return.
As if weighing the sky
On their delicate wings,
Exploring places unknown,
Crafting lasting memories.

What was that space,
So beautiful?
My dreams were alive,
And so were you.
I only knew
That I was with you.

57. AN EMPTY MIND

A blank sheet of paper
Flying aimlessly,
Wherever the wind blows,
Drifting without direction.

An empty cardboard box,
Kicked along the road,
Side by side
On a busy street,
Tossed by indifferent feet.

Sitting on the bench
In the park,
Eyes wide open,
Rolling left and right,
Watching people
Pass by meaninglessly,
No thoughts,
No feelings,
No purpose.

Just like the day,
Boring to the core,
So utterly useless,
An echo of emptiness,

A whisper of stillness,
Lost in the void.

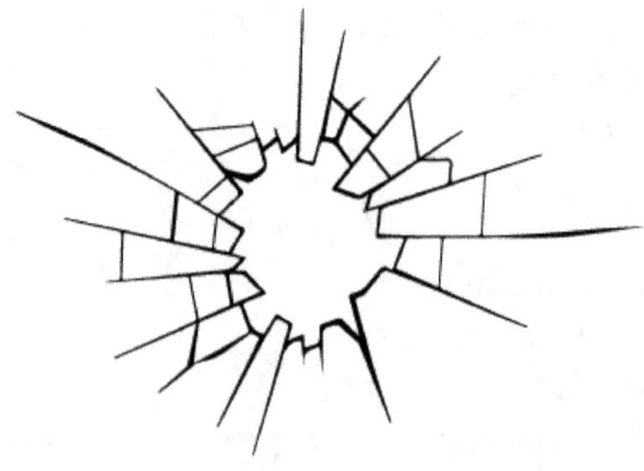

58. THE ENCOUNTER

I was on my way home,
The breeze touching my face,
Hinting something is about to happen.
My mind and body go with the flow,
Eager to feel what is in store.
But I don't know why my heart was pounding,
As if time were running away.

I had finished my day's thoughts,
When a new one knocked on my head,
Suggesting the unthinkable was near
We had met just once,
And to feel anything further
Seemed far from me and my routine.
But the restlessness wouldn't stop,
As if it wanted to explode and fly away.

I was almost there now,
With no expectations,
Nor waiting for a surprise.
For all the while, I was in exile,
Keeping my mind far away,
Distant from love, unready to give.
But there's a strange sweetness in the dusk,
Chilly, yet drawing me into its musk.

And there you come, right in front of me,
With white lilies making their way
Into my hands, shaky and uncertain,
Unable to withstand
The burden of countless thoughts
Which have suddenly come to an end
With the hope that it doesn't turn tragic.

Is this a dream or something real?
As if I am in heaven and no one is around,
Just me, and my love,
Lost in this moment's profound magic.

59. IT'S YOUR LIFE

Does it really help,
Walking a path alone,
When you know
It won't be liked?

But then, does it matter?
Whether they like it or not.
Isn't it right?
What you like, what you do.
For it's you who matters to you, not them.

You ponder and ponder alone.
Mostly, it's the other way around.
You act because they should like it,
Though you know
What you're doing, you don't like.
You realize this is the only way to pull through,
For your own mental well-being, not theirs.

Will it really sustain,
Going on a path with them?
Because when you truly need them,
They always leave you alone.
For them, it doesn't matter
What you do, what you like.

It's their selfish wants,
Their needs, their desires, they want you to
fulfill.

Does it have to be like this,
A life that is borrowed,
Not your own, not on your terms,
Lacking its sheen, dried like leaves,
Waiting to fall with the slightest blow of wind?

But indeed, it should matter,
How you see it, not them.

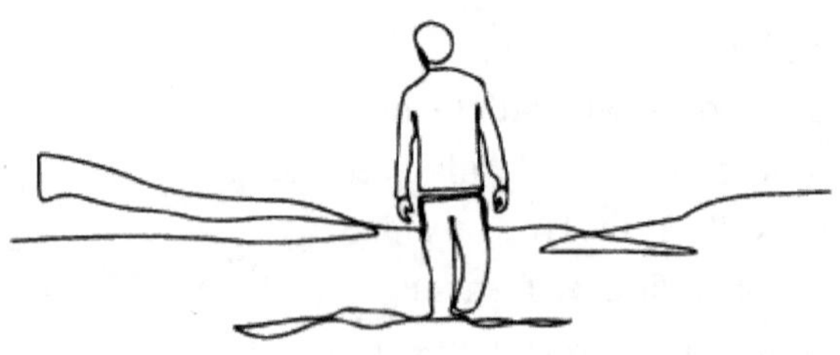

60. BROKEN HEART

It was on the table,
It fell,
It cracked,
And maybe it was already broken,
But you walked away
Without a backward glance.

This was the place
Where we sat,
We drank,
Shared our joys and sorrows,
And everything that mattered.
But you just forgot
What it meant,
Without an iota of regret.

This is where I imagined
And dreamt, about our future.
I cherished your thoughts.
You were gentle,
Just like my soul,
Making my heart sing,
And made it glow.

I wanted to keep it there,
As it lay,
Shining supreme.
I could see my reflection,
Pure and serene.

And then you came,
Abrupt,
And trampled it over,
The moment I laid my heart bare.
As if nothing were there,
On that table or anywhere,
It all disappeared
In a moment so big,
We couldn't compress it.
It gave us hope
To create a world
Full of love
Around a toughened glass.

Whoever tried
To make it weak and wreck,
We were there for each other,
With our hands around,
Protecting it forever.

And now it lies there,
In pieces and broken.
My heart weeps in anguish,

The love is forgotten.

I wish the same for you,
As you run miles away,
To forget and overcome,
But you will forever see,
Engulfed in a craving for love.
For you didn't grasp
The power of love,
And so, its destruction.

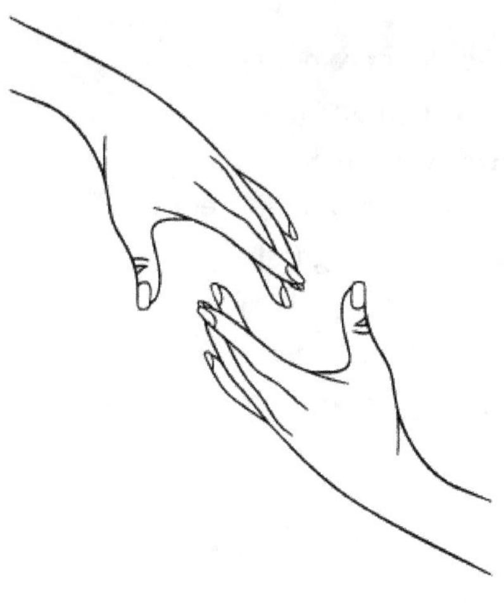

61. TIME SAILS

The abode is now laden
With heaps of dried leaves,
Mostly dust and remnants of weeps.
Windows closed,
Deprived of the breeze.
The walls, once vibrant,
Now frozen, dull, and creaking.
The doors have turned their backs,
Their color is now a sorrowful gray.
The locks refuse to stay,
And the keys are long forgotten,
Once proudly hung,
Nailed inside a visible corner.

Under the floor are buried
The chaos and noises,
Cherished with flocks.
Night and day are no different;
Silence is the only guest.
It peeps everywhere,
Seeking what it can never find.
For the time that goes
Never comes back,
To clean the dust,
Remove the blackened sheets

Covering the tables and chairs.
The sofa's railing underneath,
Waiting for someone to warm it up
And ring the bell for once,
To restore the life
Bring the chaos back
And turn the door bloody red!

62. HER WARMTH

I see her in photos and in real life,
Ever smiling, ever ready,
Beaming with a light,
A mystic energy
to continue her fight.
Her smile, her love,
All the things she cares for.
She is not far away,
But I yearn for her deeply,
And I see myself in her
As I cherish her thoughts
In this silent, lonely house.

I think she is still growing,
And suddenly, there she is
In the kitchen, giving me a hand
A sight so precious as I share
She speaks with the elderly,
Seeing deeply inside and out,
A profound care in her gentle voice,
Overflowing with patience,
Never showing boredom.
She understands me and my inner voice
She listens and talks her mind
It frees me from my woes
She has a secret door
To bring in all the love in the world,

And spreads it to everyone around.

In a world of distractions
Toys, games, and gadgets
Her list of true friends is few,
But she adores them deeply.
She finds solace in books and novels,
Her true companions.
Her dreams and poems,
She loves to read them aloud,
And her own stories carve a path
Into the souls of those around.
How I wish the world could hear,
For they come from her heart
And are truly rare.

Here's to my angel,
With all the love and blessings,
And the God almighty
Forever by your side,
In all you do!

63. NOT SO FAR AWAY

It's a secret place
To hide away my emotions
Just a shout away
And there they come
To unravel the moments
That we live for every single day.

Bold thoughts and strong shoulders,
I lean on them whenever I need support
A pat on the back when I do well
And the lame pranks when I least expect it.
In the midst of a serious thought,
A loud thud is all I hear.
They crowd around
with their laughter and cheer,
lifting my mood
and getting me where I want to be.

They hold the key to my secret place,
taking away the pain and sorrow,
filling it with happiness,
laughter, and dimes.
I talk my heart out
without any shame,
trusting them fully,

hugging them deeply,
knowing they care
for who I am.

They are just a call away,
And there we go again,
through successes and failures,
life's ups and downs,
the roller-coaster ride.

Time is running,
we see the color gray,
yet the laughter and pranks remain,
making us children once more,
riding that memory lane
together and forever,
as we dear friends meet again.

64. LIFE'S PATH

I chose good over bad,
and being meek at times rather than fierce.
For I have seen their tears
and their broken hearts.
I chose to share rather than to snatch away.

I found it better to be sane than mad,
and to work hard for success.
Climbing the ladder toward happiness,
amidst the tedious routine,
I chose the difficult path over resting away.

I believed in tasting the tears,
discovering their bitterness,
and admitting they do not taste sweet.
The roads are rough, the journey, tedious,
but I picked faith over doubt,
trusting the sun will pierce
the thickest clouds the earth ever stretched.
I meant to be rather than not to be,
in moments that die in a blink of a second.
For I have known hunger and the miles sought,
understanding that after the last, returns the first.
And despite what others say, you mustn't retreat.

I chose to go on,
for I don't know how to give up
when life tricks me.
Life's lessons are the dreams,
not the ones woven in a brittle click.
For there is only one way
to come into this world
and make your presence felt,
but there are many ways to leave it.

65. FACE IT

I giggled it away,
It came naturally
To overlook life's sorrows.

I hunted for little things
That gave me peace,
A reason to cheer,
To celebrate, to laugh
At life's doings,
Which you never asked for,
They just came your way.

A broken childhood
And the scars
that left their mark,
To accept what is and see
Life as a guest
At your behest.

Treat it well,
Feed it with positive thoughts,
For someone once said
Experience it is
It will come wrapped
As a gift for endurance.

I ignored it away,
The small setbacks,
Those moments
When you felt broke,
Stuck, unable to breathe.

Escaping that sheer hell
Was a difficult task you knew,
Face it as it comes,
Go with the flow.
Don't keep high hopes,
Do your best
And leave the rest.

For someone once said,
"There is light after dark",
And when you're on top,
You will see, in a matter of time
You will go down.
Nothing is permanent,
Not even your mood.

So don't be a sunken lad,
Let the tears mingle with the rain
For there will be sunlight after that,
And a rainbow to cheer you bright.

66. OH DEATH!

Oh Death, why do you come?
I know you well,
You have visited us many times.
Once, when my Granny told me
She was waiting for someone to arrive.
I was so sure no one would come,
We would play with her all day
Always around, not leaving her long.
And then, one day, those weary hands
Suddenly disappeared…
Who fed us when Mom was ill,
And my hair went dry without the oil.

Why do you come so frequently?
You came when I wanted him to stay
A bit longer, I'd say,
For happiness had just arrived.
There was a bounty after hard toil,
I wanted him around…
My favorite uncle, whose big smile
Filled everyone's heart.
Our accomplishments were his,
The biggest for him.
He would turn into a radio,
Broadcasting for the people to know
What we had done for the world to see.

And in the blink of an eye, he was gone,
Surrounded in your arms.
Now it's all dry and meaningless
without his charm.

This is a long life, I was certain,
At least for my mother, who was quieter now,
With the names of the gods in her books,
Determined to engrave them on her lips.
Living her life fully, each and every day,
Her simple and complaint-free ways
She looked forward,
For yet another day.
With her grand-children
Filling her days.

And there you came,
With your mighty chariot,
To lift her from the heavy burdens
Of life and its people,
Of the pain and agony
Which she endured, secretly, alone.
As if you wanted to show her
What she has missed
in a place where only she could see
With you around and those you took
Is that what it's meant, you say?

Then again you came.

Couldn't you wait a little longer?
When the black and white shades
Turned into bright colors—
Red, yellow, blue, and green,
Orange and purple to fill my home—
I'd think now is when
My father could rest a little
At my abode,
With his stories yet to be heard.

He was pleased with what he saw,
Rested in peace with a deep sigh,
And wanted us to visit the places, together
Of mountains and snows,
Where he brought us to this earth.
But you had no patience,
Taking him so quickly
To the skies where he didn't belong,
And left me to wander and to weep.
What is life
Without the ones we love
And care so deeply!!

67. SEARCH

I feel lost among people,
Searching for my soul.
Tell me my purpose, I'd ask,
Entangled in my own thoughts,
Looking for the true beings
Who need nothing,
From this life, and from me.

I feel betrayed in places
Full of people I once believed
Were my lifeline,
Whom I cherished,
To whom I gave my sweat and blood,
Sacrificing my space, my family time,
For what, I'd often ask.
It's not what really happens
That hurts so much,
But the opinions of what is said
About what happens.

Then I see the smile on children's faces,
The innocence in animals' eyes,
The plants grow
when you feed them well.
They give you things you didn't even ask for,

Filling you with moments of joy,
Food for your soul,
Calmness for your mind,
And your heart swells with
Love and pride.

I have found life's purpose:
To live and let live,
For you live life but once.
Make the best of what you have.
Gain all the wisdom that our elders said
Live simply. Dream big.
Be grateful.
Give Love and Laugh Lots!

68. YOU, MY ANGEL

In the wintertime,
I long for summertime.
In the summertime,
I yearn for wintertime.
When I'm in the mountains,
I crave the sea.
When I'm at the seashore,
I miss the mountain winds
Whispering through the peaks.

In the daytime,
I cherish the evenings.
In the evenings,
I adore the daytime.
Why is it that sometimes
The dusk looks beautiful,
And then I miss the dawn?

But you, my angel,
I love you anytime,
Every time.

69. FRIENDS

Just being friends is all it needs,
Hold it tight towards your heart,
Come what may, don't let it part.
These lives are precious,
Don't let them go.
Go out and hunt the things you like,
Live those moments of fun and frolic,
The stories you want to act out again,
And preserve them for what they are.

Everything we say and do
Lightens up our moods.
We can talk about whatever we want,
No strings attached, no one to stop,
No one to judge or bring us down,
Jealousy is tucked inside the box.

Just being friends is life's reward,
To lift each other when in need,
To relieve the pain no one else can see.
Together is the term we often cling to,
When we all meet, the birds do sing,
Humming our songs that we crave,
Creating that music for us to dance,
And we keep humming even as we depart.

This bond is special,
Protect it for what it's worth,
For there are people around,
Waiting to tear you apart.
Don't hold a grudge,
Go, give a hug.
Forgive is the word,
And let the world envy,
Your friendship is the key.

Filling up the alley,
Lighter than the air.
So many things tucked in the heart
Come out easily, running up the shore.
This is the team you want them to hear,
Open your mind and be by their side.
Laugh and cry, get out of despair.
What is life, if not this?
Create moments to cherish,
And among all the treasures,
This is what you want to keep.

70. THE ROUTINE

I like the routine,
and also, to see the 'not' of it,
the randomness of life
is what I admire.
Why should it be what you know
and anticipate?
Let there be chaos at times—
life's ups and downs
are what make life itself.
I like what we can see
and also, what we cannot,
and what we will not.

I like the routine,
and also, to see what it entails,
and what it cannot.
It's so much fun to just be,
to do whatever you want
is what I like to believe.
Why should you crave
and be desperate?
When you want and you get it,
be happy;
when you don't, be better off.
Be grateful,

for there's someone to protect,
to love and be loved.

Let there be no road ahead,
for it makes you pause,
enjoy the moment—
reflect and re-examine
cherish, touch, and feel.
This is what you truly are meant for.
What's the point in running endlessly
when you can live just another day?

71. PAGES OF A DIARY

Who knows what must have happened,
the writing is a mess—
as if the hand had no strength,
or the ink ran dry.
Did the day pass without food?
No friend to call,
no one to cry with.
There is no ending.

Who knows why the pages seem wet,
the writing soaked with tears and loneliness—
as if screaming for the box to be opened,
for the curtains to be drawn aside.
Where is the magic?
Where is the light?
No window in these four walls,
no soul that feels alive.
There is no room.

Who knows why some drawings are left
incomplete,
the pages worn out, pale, and yellow.
And then a backward glance—
to the same scribbles on the next few pages.

There are dried leaves and petals,
perhaps remnants of memories.
Thoughts but no feelings,
plenty of words but no meaning.
No real people,
no real things.
There is no poem.

* 9 7 8 9 3 6 3 3 1 7 8 9 5 *